50 Delicious Abroad Noodle Dishes

By: Kelly Johnson

Table of Contents

- Pad Thai (Thailand)
- Pho (Vietnam)
- Ramen (Japan)
- Laksa (Malaysia/Singapore)
- Soba Noodles (Japan)
- Chow Mein (China)
- Spaghetti Aglio e Olio (Italy)
- Pad See Ew (Thailand)
- Udon (Japan)
- Bun Cha (Vietnam)
- Jajangmyeon (South Korea)
- Dan Dan Noodles (China)
- Mee Goreng (Malaysia/Indonesia)
- Kuy Teav (Cambodia)
- Zhajiangmian (China)
- Wonton Noodles (Hong Kong)
- Pho Bo (Vietnam)

- Banh Canh (Vietnam)
- Mian (China)
- Tom Yum Noodles (Thailand)
- Kuy Tieu (Vietnam)
- Fideuà (Spain)
- Sapporo Miso Ramen (Japan)
- Chilled Noodles with Sesame Sauce (China)
- Cantonese Noodles (Hong Kong)
- Soba Noodles with Tempura (Japan)
- Mee Rebus (Malaysia)
- Cold Noodles with Cucumber (China)
- Tantanmen (Japan)
- Drunken Noodles (Thailand)
- Khao Soi (Thailand)
- Japchae (South Korea)
- Pho Ga (Vietnam)
- Char Kway Teow (Malaysia)
- Yaki Soba (Japan)
- Beef Noodle Soup (Taiwan)

- Noodle Soup with Pork (China)
- Mie Ayam (Indonesia)
- Baked Ziti (Italy)
- Yakisoba (Japan)
- Sweet Soy Noodles (Indonesia)
- Stir-Fried Rice Noodles with Shrimp (Vietnam)
- Khao Poon (Laos)
- Spaghetti Carbonara (Italy)
- Guo Tie Noodles (China)
- Noodle Soup with Fish Balls (Hong Kong)
- Singapore Noodles (Singapore)
- Xian Biang Biang Noodles (China)
- Kuy Teav Phnom Penh (Cambodia)
- Laksa Lemak (Malaysia)

Pad Thai (Thailand)
Ingredients:

- 8 oz rice noodles
- 2 tbsp vegetable oil
- 1/2 lb shrimp, peeled and deveined (or tofu for a vegetarian version)
- 2 eggs, lightly beaten
- 1/2 cup bean sprouts
- 1/4 cup chopped green onions
- 1/4 cup crushed peanuts
- 1 lime, cut into wedges
- 1 tbsp brown sugar
- 2 tbsp fish sauce
- 1 tbsp soy sauce
- 1 tbsp tamarind paste
- 1/2 tsp chili flakes
- 2 cloves garlic, minced
- 1 tbsp vegetable oil
- Fresh cilantro for garnish

Instructions:

1. Cook the rice noodles according to package instructions. Drain and set aside.

2. In a small bowl, whisk together fish sauce, soy sauce, tamarind paste, brown sugar, and chili flakes. Set aside.

3. Heat vegetable oil in a wok or large pan over medium-high heat. Add shrimp (or tofu) and cook for 2-3 minutes, until pink and cooked through. Remove from the pan and set aside.

4. Add garlic and cook until fragrant. Push to the side of the pan.

5. Pour in beaten eggs and scramble until cooked.

6. Add noodles, sauce, shrimp/tofu, bean sprouts, and green onions. Toss to combine.

7. Serve with crushed peanuts, lime wedges, and cilantro.

Pho (Vietnam)

Ingredients:

- 1 lb beef brisket or chicken (or both)
- 2 onions, halved
- 2-inch piece of ginger, sliced
- 3-4 star anise
- 2 cinnamon sticks
- 4-5 cloves
- 1 tsp coriander seeds
- 2 tbsp fish sauce
- 1 tbsp sugar
- 1 tbsp soy sauce
- 8 cups beef or chicken broth
- 8 oz rice noodles
- Fresh herbs (cilantro, basil, mint)
- Bean sprouts
- Lime wedges
- Sriracha and hoisin sauce (optional)

Instructions:

1. Char onions and ginger by placing them directly on a burner or broiling in the oven until blackened.

2. In a large pot, add beef or chicken, charred onions, ginger, star anise, cinnamon sticks, cloves, and coriander seeds. Cover with broth and bring to a boil.

3. Lower the heat and simmer for about 1-2 hours for beef (30 minutes for chicken), skimming off any foam.

4. Remove the beef or chicken from the broth and set aside. Strain the broth to remove solid ingredients.

5. Cook the rice noodles according to package instructions.

6. Slice the beef thinly (if using).

7. Assemble the pho by placing noodles in bowls, adding sliced beef/chicken, and pouring hot broth over the top.

8. Serve with fresh herbs, bean sprouts, lime wedges, and optional sauces.

Ramen (Japan)
Ingredients:

- 4 cups chicken or pork broth
- 2 tbsp soy sauce
- 1 tbsp miso paste
- 1 tbsp sesame oil
- 2 cloves garlic, minced
- 2 boiled eggs, halved
- 1/2 cup corn kernels (optional)
- 2 green onions, sliced
- 4 oz ramen noodles
- 1/2 cup spinach or bok choy (optional)
- 1/2 cup cooked pork belly or chicken (optional)
- Nori (seaweed) for garnish

Instructions:

1. Heat sesame oil in a pot and sauté garlic until fragrant.
2. Add broth, soy sauce, and miso paste, and bring to a simmer.
3. Cook ramen noodles according to package instructions.
4. Divide the noodles into bowls. Pour the hot broth over the noodles.

5. Top with boiled eggs, green onions, spinach/bok choy, corn, and pork belly/chicken.

6. Garnish with nori and serve hot.

Laksa (Malaysia/Singapore)

Ingredients:

- 200g rice noodles
- 1 tbsp vegetable oil
- 2 tbsp red curry paste
- 1 can (400ml) coconut milk
- 3 cups chicken broth
- 1 tbsp fish sauce
- 2 tbsp lime juice
- 200g cooked chicken, shredded
- 2 boiled eggs, halved
- Fresh cilantro and mint for garnish
- Bean sprouts and sliced chili for garnish

Instructions:

1. Cook rice noodles according to package instructions.
2. In a large pot, heat vegetable oil and sauté red curry paste until fragrant.
3. Add coconut milk, chicken broth, fish sauce, and lime juice. Bring to a boil.
4. Simmer for 10 minutes, then add shredded chicken.
5. Divide the noodles into bowls and pour the hot broth over the noodles.
6. Top with boiled eggs, cilantro, mint, bean sprouts, and chili slices. Serve hot.

Soba Noodles (Japan)

Ingredients:

- 8 oz soba noodles
- 2 tbsp soy sauce
- 1 tbsp mirin
- 1 tbsp sesame oil
- 1 tsp rice vinegar
- 1 tbsp chopped green onions
- 1/2 tsp sesame seeds
- 1/2 cucumber, julienned (optional)
- 1 boiled egg (optional)

Instructions:

1. Cook soba noodles according to package instructions. Drain and rinse with cold water.
2. In a small bowl, mix soy sauce, mirin, sesame oil, and rice vinegar.
3. Toss the soba noodles with the sauce mixture.
4. Garnish with green onions, sesame seeds, cucumber, and boiled egg (if using). Serve chilled or at room temperature.

Chow Mein (China)

Ingredients:

- 8 oz chow mein noodles
- 2 tbsp vegetable oil
- 1/2 lb chicken breast, thinly sliced
- 1 bell pepper, thinly sliced
- 1 carrot, julienned
- 1 onion, sliced
- 2 cloves garlic, minced
- 3 tbsp soy sauce
- 1 tbsp oyster sauce
- 1 tbsp hoisin sauce
- 1/4 tsp black pepper

Instructions:

1. Cook chow mein noodles according to package instructions. Drain and set aside.
2. Heat vegetable oil in a wok or large pan. Add chicken and cook until browned.
3. Add garlic, onion, bell pepper, and carrot. Cook for 3-4 minutes, until vegetables are tender.
4. Add noodles to the pan and toss with soy sauce, oyster sauce, hoisin sauce, and black pepper.
5. Stir-fry for 2-3 minutes until everything is combined and heated through.

6. Serve hot.

Spaghetti Aglio e Olio (Italy)
Ingredients:

- 8 oz spaghetti
- 4 cloves garlic, thinly sliced
- 1/4 cup olive oil
- 1/4 tsp red pepper flakes
- Salt and pepper
- Fresh parsley, chopped
- Grated Parmesan cheese (optional)

Instructions:

1. Cook spaghetti according to package instructions. Drain, reserving some pasta water.
2. In a large pan, heat olive oil over medium heat. Add garlic and red pepper flakes. Sauté until garlic is golden brown.
3. Add cooked spaghetti to the pan and toss with the garlic and oil mixture. If needed, add a splash of reserved pasta water to help combine.
4. Season with salt and pepper.
5. Garnish with fresh parsley and Parmesan cheese (optional). Serve immediately.

Pad See Ew (Thailand)

Ingredients:

- 8 oz wide rice noodles
- 2 tbsp vegetable oil
- 1/2 lb chicken, beef, or pork, thinly sliced
- 2 eggs, lightly beaten
- 1/2 cup broccoli or Chinese broccoli
- 3 tbsp soy sauce
- 1 tbsp dark soy sauce
- 1 tbsp sugar
- 1/2 tsp black pepper
- Fresh lime wedges

Instructions:

1. Cook rice noodles according to package instructions. Drain and set aside.
2. Heat vegetable oil in a wok or large pan. Add chicken (or other protein) and cook until browned.
3. Push the protein to one side and add eggs. Scramble until cooked.
4. Add noodles, soy sauces, sugar, black pepper, and broccoli. Toss to combine.
5. Serve with lime wedges.

Udon (Japan)
Ingredients:

- 8 oz udon noodles
- 4 cups dashi (Japanese soup stock)
- 2 tbsp soy sauce
- 1 tbsp mirin
- 1 tbsp sugar
- 1/2 cup green onions, chopped
- 1/2 sheet nori, shredded (optional)
- Tofu or tempura for garnish (optional)

Instructions:

1. Cook udon noodles according to package instructions. Drain and set aside.
2. In a pot, combine dashi, soy sauce, mirin, and sugar. Bring to a simmer.
3. Divide cooked udon noodles into bowls and pour hot broth over the noodles.
4. Top with green onions, nori, and optional tofu or tempura. Serve hot.

Bun Cha (Vietnam)

Ingredients:

- 1 lb ground pork
- 2 tbsp fish sauce
- 1 tbsp sugar
- 1/2 tsp black pepper
- 1 clove garlic, minced
- 1 small onion, finely chopped
- Fresh herbs (cilantro, mint, Thai basil)
- 1 cucumber, julienned
- Rice vermicelli noodles
- Pickled vegetables (optional)

Instructions:

1. In a bowl, mix ground pork, fish sauce, sugar, black pepper, garlic, and onion. Form into small patties.
2. Grill or pan-fry the patties until cooked through.
3. Cook rice vermicelli noodles according to package instructions.
4. To serve, place noodles in bowls and top with patties, fresh herbs, cucumber, and optional pickled vegetables.
5. Serve with dipping sauce.

Jajangmyeon (South Korea)
Ingredients:

- 8 oz wheat noodles
- 1 lb pork belly or ground pork
- 1 onion, chopped
- 1 zucchini, chopped
- 1/2 cup fermented black bean paste (chunjang)
- 2 tbsp soy sauce
- 1 tbsp sugar
- 2 cups chicken broth
- 2 tbsp vegetable oil
- 1 tbsp cornstarch mixed with 2 tbsp water
- 1/2 cup cucumber, julienned (for garnish)

Instructions:

1. Cook wheat noodles according to package instructions. Drain and set aside.
2. Heat vegetable oil in a pan over medium-high heat. Add pork and cook until browned.
3. Add onion and zucchini, cooking until soft.
4. Stir in the black bean paste and soy sauce, then add the sugar.
5. Pour in the chicken broth and bring to a simmer.

6. Stir in the cornstarch mixture to thicken the sauce.

7. Serve the sauce over the noodles and garnish with julienned cucumber.

Dan Dan Noodles (China)

Ingredients:

- 8 oz Chinese wheat noodles
- 1/2 lb ground pork
- 2 tbsp sesame paste (or peanut butter)
- 2 tbsp soy sauce
- 1 tbsp rice vinegar
- 1 tbsp chili oil
- 2 tsp sugar
- 2 cloves garlic, minced
- 1 tbsp ginger, minced
- 1/2 cup chopped green onions
- 1 tbsp Sichuan peppercorns, ground (optional)
- 1/4 cup chopped cilantro (optional)

Instructions:

1. Cook noodles according to package instructions. Drain and set aside.
2. In a pan, cook ground pork over medium heat until browned.
3. Add garlic and ginger, cooking until fragrant.
4. Stir in sesame paste, soy sauce, rice vinegar, chili oil, and sugar. Mix well.
5. Toss the cooked noodles in the sauce, making sure they're well coated.

6. Top with green onions, Sichuan peppercorns, and cilantro. Serve hot.

Mee Goreng (Malaysia/Indonesia)
Ingredients:

- 8 oz yellow noodles
- 2 tbsp vegetable oil
- 1/2 lb shrimp or chicken, sliced
- 1 onion, sliced
- 1/2 cup cabbage, shredded
- 2 eggs, scrambled
- 2 tbsp sweet soy sauce (kecap manis)
- 1 tbsp soy sauce
- 1 tbsp chili paste
- 1 tbsp sugar
- 1/2 tsp turmeric powder
- 1/2 tsp paprika
- 1/4 cup bean sprouts
- 1/4 cup chopped green onions

Instructions:

1. Cook noodles according to package instructions. Drain and set aside.
2. Heat oil in a wok or large pan over medium-high heat. Add shrimp/chicken and cook until browned.

3. Add onion, cabbage, and scrambled eggs. Stir-fry until vegetables are tender.

4. Stir in sweet soy sauce, soy sauce, chili paste, sugar, turmeric, and paprika.

5. Add noodles and toss to coat in the sauce.

6. Top with bean sprouts and green onions. Serve hot.

Kuy Teav (Cambodia)

Ingredients:

- 8 oz rice noodles
- 1/2 lb ground beef or pork
- 2 tbsp fish sauce
- 1 tbsp soy sauce
- 2 tbsp sugar
- 2 cloves garlic, minced
- 1/4 cup cilantro, chopped
- 2 boiled eggs, halved
- 1/2 cup bean sprouts
- 1 lime, cut into wedges

Instructions:

1. Cook rice noodles according to package instructions. Drain and set aside.
2. In a pan, cook ground beef or pork until browned. Add garlic and cook until fragrant.
3. Stir in fish sauce, soy sauce, and sugar.
4. Serve noodles in bowls and top with the cooked meat mixture, boiled eggs, cilantro, and bean sprouts.
5. Garnish with lime wedges. Serve hot.

Zhajiangmian (China)

Ingredients:

- 8 oz Chinese wheat noodles
- 1/2 lb ground pork
- 2 tbsp fermented soybean paste (or hoisin sauce)
- 1 tbsp soy sauce
- 1/2 cup chicken broth
- 2 tbsp vegetable oil
- 2 cloves garlic, minced
- 1/4 cup cucumber, julienned
- 1/4 cup shredded carrots
- 2 tbsp green onions, chopped

Instructions:

1. Cook wheat noodles according to package instructions. Drain and set aside.
2. Heat vegetable oil in a pan over medium heat. Add ground pork and cook until browned.
3. Add garlic and cook until fragrant.
4. Stir in fermented soybean paste, soy sauce, and chicken broth. Bring to a simmer.
5. Serve the sauce over the noodles and garnish with cucumber, carrots, and green onions.

Wonton Noodles (Hong Kong)
Ingredients:

- 8 oz egg noodles
- 12-15 wontons (store-bought or homemade)
- 4 cups chicken broth
- 2 tbsp soy sauce
- 1 tbsp oyster sauce
- 1 tsp sesame oil
- 1/4 cup chopped green onions
- 1 tbsp bok choy or spinach (optional)

Instructions:

1. Cook egg noodles according to package instructions. Drain and set aside.
2. In a pot, bring chicken broth to a boil. Add soy sauce, oyster sauce, and sesame oil.
3. Add the wontons and cook until they float to the top (about 5 minutes).
4. Divide noodles into bowls and pour the hot broth and wontons over the noodles.
5. Garnish with green onions and bok choy/spinach.

Pho Bo (Vietnam)

Ingredients:

- 1 lb beef (brisket, sirloin, or flank steak)
- 8 oz rice noodles
- 4 cups beef broth
- 2 onions, halved
- 2-inch piece ginger, sliced
- 3-4 star anise
- 2 cinnamon sticks
- 1 tbsp fish sauce
- 1 tbsp soy sauce
- Fresh herbs (basil, cilantro, mint)
- Bean sprouts, lime wedges, and chili slices for garnish

Instructions:

1. Char onions and ginger by broiling or charring on a gas burner.
2. In a pot, add beef, charred onions, ginger, star anise, cinnamon sticks, fish sauce, and soy sauce. Cover with beef broth and bring to a boil.
3. Lower heat and simmer for about 1-2 hours, skimming off any impurities.
4. Slice the beef thinly.
5. Cook rice noodles according to package instructions.

6. Assemble pho by placing noodles in bowls and topping with sliced beef and hot broth.

7. Garnish with herbs, bean sprouts, lime, and chili slices.

Banh Canh (Vietnam)

Ingredients:

- 8 oz banh canh noodles (or thick rice noodles)
- 1 lb shrimp or fish cakes
- 4 cups chicken or pork broth
- 2 tbsp fish sauce
- 1 tbsp sugar
- 1/2 tsp black pepper
- 2 cloves garlic, minced
- 1/4 cup chopped green onions
- Fresh herbs (cilantro, Thai basil)

Instructions:

1. Cook the banh canh noodles according to package instructions. Drain and set aside.
2. In a pot, heat broth, fish sauce, sugar, and black pepper. Bring to a simmer.
3. Add shrimp or fish cakes and cook until tender.
4. Add cooked noodles to the soup and simmer for 3-4 minutes.
5. Garnish with green onions and fresh herbs. Serve hot.

Mian (China)

Ingredients:

- 8 oz Chinese wheat noodles
- 1/2 lb ground pork or chicken
- 2 tbsp soy sauce
- 1 tbsp rice vinegar
- 1 tbsp sesame oil
- 1 tbsp sugar
- 2 cloves garlic, minced
- 2 tbsp green onions, chopped
- 1/4 tsp chili flakes (optional)

Instructions:

1. Cook noodles according to package instructions. Drain and set aside.
2. Heat sesame oil in a pan over medium-high heat. Add ground pork or chicken and cook until browned.
3. Add garlic and cook until fragrant.
4. Stir in soy sauce, rice vinegar, and sugar.
5. Toss noodles in the sauce mixture and stir to combine.
6. Garnish with green onions and chili flakes (optional).

Tom Yum Noodles (Thailand)
Ingredients:

- 8 oz rice noodles
- 4 cups chicken or vegetable broth
- 2 tbsp fish sauce
- 1 tbsp lime juice
- 1 tbsp sugar
- 2-3 kaffir lime leaves, torn
- 1 stalk lemongrass, smashed
- 2-3 Thai bird chilies, smashed
- 1/2 lb shrimp (optional)
- Fresh cilantro for garnish

Instructions:

1. Cook noodles according to package instructions. Drain and set aside.
2. In a pot, bring the broth to a boil. Add fish sauce, lime juice, sugar, kaffir lime leaves, lemongrass, and bird chilies.
3. Add shrimp (if using) and cook until pink.
4. Add noodles to the pot and stir to combine.
5. Garnish with fresh cilantro and serve hot.

Kuy Tieu (Vietnam)
Ingredients:

- 8 oz rice noodles
- 1 lb shrimp or ground pork
- 1/2 cup fish sauce
- 2 tbsp soy sauce
- 1 tbsp sugar
- 1 tsp black pepper
- 2 cloves garlic, minced
- 1/4 cup cilantro, chopped
- 1 lime, cut into wedges
- 1/4 cup bean sprouts
- 1/4 cup chopped green onions

Instructions:

1. Cook rice noodles according to package instructions. Drain and set aside.
2. In a pot, cook shrimp or ground pork over medium heat until browned.
3. Add garlic, fish sauce, soy sauce, sugar, and black pepper. Stir to combine.
4. Pour in enough water or broth to cover the meat and bring to a boil.
5. Add cooked noodles to the pot and stir to combine.

6. Serve in bowls and garnish with cilantro, lime wedges, bean sprouts, and green onions.

Fideuà (Spain)
Ingredients:

- 8 oz short pasta (fideuà noodles or vermicelli)
- 1 lb seafood (shrimp, squid, clams, etc.)
- 1 onion, chopped
- 2 cloves garlic, minced
- 1 red bell pepper, chopped
- 2 tomatoes, grated
- 2 tbsp olive oil
- 4 cups fish or seafood broth
- 1/2 tsp saffron threads
- 1/2 tsp smoked paprika
- Salt and pepper to taste
- Lemon wedges for garnish

Instructions:

1. Heat olive oil in a large pan over medium heat. Add onion, garlic, and bell pepper and cook until soft.
2. Stir in the grated tomatoes, saffron, smoked paprika, salt, and pepper.
3. Add the seafood and cook until tender.
4. Stir in the pasta, followed by the broth. Bring to a simmer and cook until the pasta is tender and the liquid has absorbed.

5. Serve with lemon wedges for garnish.

Sapporo Miso Ramen (Japan)

Ingredients:

- 4 cups chicken broth
- 2 tbsp miso paste
- 1 tbsp soy sauce
- 1 tbsp sesame oil
- 2 packs ramen noodles
- 1/2 lb ground pork
- 1/4 cup green onions, chopped
- 2 boiled eggs
- 1 tbsp butter (optional)
- Corn and bamboo shoots (optional)

Instructions:

1. In a pot, heat sesame oil and cook ground pork until browned.
2. Add miso paste, soy sauce, and chicken broth. Stir to combine and bring to a simmer.
3. Meanwhile, cook ramen noodles according to package instructions. Drain and set aside.
4. Add butter to the broth for richness (optional).
5. Serve the ramen noodles in bowls, pour the broth over them, and top with boiled eggs, green onions, corn, and bamboo shoots.

Chilled Noodles with Sesame Sauce (China)

Ingredients:

- 8 oz wheat noodles
- 3 tbsp tahini or sesame paste
- 1 tbsp soy sauce
- 1 tbsp rice vinegar
- 1 tbsp sugar
- 1 tbsp sesame oil
- 1/4 tsp chili oil (optional)
- 2 cloves garlic, minced
- 1/4 cup chopped green onions
- Cucumber, julienned (for garnish)

Instructions:

1. Cook noodles according to package instructions. Drain and rinse with cold water to chill.
2. In a bowl, mix tahini, soy sauce, rice vinegar, sugar, sesame oil, chili oil, and garlic to make the sauce.
3. Toss the chilled noodles in the sesame sauce and combine thoroughly.
4. Garnish with green onions and julienned cucumber. Serve cold.

Cantonese Noodles (Hong Kong)

Ingredients:

- 8 oz egg noodles
- 1/2 lb shrimp, peeled and deveined
- 1/2 lb chicken breast, sliced
- 2 tbsp oyster sauce
- 1 tbsp soy sauce
- 1 tbsp hoisin sauce
- 1 tbsp sesame oil
- 2 cloves garlic, minced
- 1/4 cup green onions, chopped

Instructions:

1. Cook the egg noodles according to package instructions. Drain and set aside.
2. In a wok, heat sesame oil over medium heat. Add garlic, chicken, and shrimp. Stir-fry until cooked through.
3. Stir in oyster sauce, soy sauce, and hoisin sauce.
4. Add cooked noodles and toss to coat in the sauce.
5. Garnish with chopped green onions. Serve hot.

Soba Noodles with Tempura (Japan)

Ingredients:

- 8 oz soba noodles
- 1/2 cup shrimp or vegetable tempura (store-bought or homemade)
- 4 cups dashi (broth)
- 2 tbsp soy sauce
- 1 tbsp mirin
- 1 tbsp sesame oil
- 2 boiled eggs, sliced
- 1/4 cup green onions, chopped
- Sesame seeds for garnish

Instructions:

1. Cook soba noodles according to package instructions. Drain and set aside.
2. In a pot, heat dashi, soy sauce, mirin, and sesame oil to make the broth. Bring to a simmer.
3. Serve noodles in bowls and pour the broth over them.
4. Top with tempura, boiled eggs, green onions, and sesame seeds.

Mee Rebus (Malaysia)

Ingredients:

- 8 oz yellow noodles
- 1/2 lb shrimp or chicken
- 2 tbsp curry powder
- 2 tbsp tomato paste
- 2 tbsp soy sauce
- 1 tbsp sugar
- 1/2 cup bean sprouts
- 1 boiled egg, halved
- 1/4 cup chopped green onions

Instructions:

1. Cook yellow noodles according to package instructions. Drain and set aside.
2. In a pot, cook shrimp or chicken until tender.
3. Add curry powder, tomato paste, soy sauce, and sugar. Stir to combine.
4. Add enough water or broth to make a sauce. Bring to a simmer.
5. Serve noodles in bowls and pour the sauce over. Garnish with bean sprouts, boiled egg, and green onions.

Cold Noodles with Cucumber (China)

Ingredients:

- 8 oz wheat noodles
- 1 cucumber, julienned
- 1/4 cup soy sauce
- 1 tbsp rice vinegar
- 1 tbsp sesame oil
- 1 tsp sugar
- 2 cloves garlic, minced
- 1/4 cup green onions, chopped

Instructions:

1. Cook noodles according to package instructions. Drain and rinse with cold water to chill.
2. In a bowl, mix soy sauce, rice vinegar, sesame oil, sugar, and garlic to make the sauce.
3. Toss the chilled noodles in the sauce.
4. Garnish with julienned cucumber and green onions. Serve cold.

Tantanmen (Japan)

Ingredients:

- 8 oz ramen noodles
- 1/2 lb ground pork
- 2 tbsp sesame paste
- 1 tbsp soy sauce
- 1 tbsp rice vinegar
- 1 tbsp chili oil
- 2 cloves garlic, minced
- 2 tbsp chopped green onions
- 1 boiled egg, sliced

Instructions:

1. Cook ramen noodles according to package instructions. Drain and set aside.
2. In a pan, cook ground pork until browned.
3. Add sesame paste, soy sauce, rice vinegar, and chili oil. Stir to combine.
4. Serve noodles in bowls and top with the pork mixture, boiled egg, and green onions.

Drunken Noodles (Thailand)

Ingredients:

- 8 oz wide rice noodles
- 1/2 lb chicken or shrimp
- 1 bell pepper, sliced
- 2 cloves garlic, minced
- 1 tbsp soy sauce
- 1 tbsp fish sauce
- 1 tbsp oyster sauce
- 1 tbsp sugar
- 1 tbsp chili paste
- 1/2 cup Thai basil leaves

Instructions:

1. Cook rice noodles according to package instructions. Drain and set aside.
2. Heat oil in a pan over medium heat. Add garlic, chicken, and bell pepper. Stir-fry until cooked through.
3. Stir in soy sauce, fish sauce, oyster sauce, sugar, and chili paste.
4. Add noodles and toss to coat in the sauce.
5. Top with fresh Thai basil leaves. Serve hot.

Khao Soi (Thailand)

Ingredients:

- 8 oz egg noodles
- 1 lb chicken thighs, bone-in
- 2 tbsp red curry paste
- 1 can coconut milk
- 4 cups chicken broth
- 2 tbsp fish sauce
- 1 tbsp soy sauce
- 1 tbsp sugar
- 1/4 cup lime juice
- 1/4 cup chopped cilantro
- 1/4 cup pickled mustard greens (optional)
- Fried noodles for topping
- 1 onion, thinly sliced
- 2 cloves garlic, minced

Instructions:

1. In a large pot, sauté onion and garlic until softened. Add red curry paste and cook for 2 minutes.

2. Add chicken thighs, coconut milk, chicken broth, fish sauce, soy sauce, and sugar. Bring to a simmer and cook until chicken is tender (about 30 minutes).

3. Remove the chicken and shred it. Set aside.

4. Cook egg noodles according to package instructions.

5. To serve, place cooked noodles in bowls, add chicken and broth, and top with fried noodles, cilantro, pickled mustard greens, and lime juice.

Japchae (South Korea)
Ingredients:

- 8 oz sweet potato noodles (dangmyeon)
- 1/2 lb beef (ribeye or sirloin), thinly sliced
- 1 onion, sliced
- 1 carrot, julienned
- 1 bell pepper, sliced
- 2 cloves garlic, minced
- 2 tbsp soy sauce
- 1 tbsp sesame oil
- 1 tbsp sugar
- 1 tbsp vegetable oil
- 1 tbsp sesame seeds
- 2 eggs, scrambled (optional)

Instructions:

1. Cook the sweet potato noodles according to package instructions. Drain and rinse with cold water.

2. In a pan, sauté garlic, onion, and carrots in vegetable oil until softened. Add bell pepper and cook for 2 minutes more.

3. In another pan, sauté the beef until browned, then add soy sauce, sesame oil, and sugar.

4. In a large bowl, combine the noodles, vegetables, and beef. Toss to combine.

5. Garnish with sesame seeds and scrambled eggs (optional). Serve hot.

Pho Ga (Vietnam)

Ingredients:

- 8 oz rice noodles
- 1 lb chicken breasts
- 1 onion, quartered
- 1 piece ginger, 2-inch, sliced
- 3-4 star anise
- 2 cloves
- 1 tbsp fish sauce
- 1 tbsp soy sauce
- 1 cinnamon stick
- 1 tbsp sugar
- 4 cups chicken broth
- 1/4 cup chopped cilantro
- Lime wedges, Thai basil, and bean sprouts for garnish

Instructions:

1. In a pot, combine chicken, onion, ginger, star anise, cinnamon stick, and cloves. Add chicken broth, soy sauce, fish sauce, and sugar. Bring to a simmer and cook for 30-40 minutes.

2. Remove the chicken and shred it. Strain the broth to remove the spices.

3. Cook rice noodles according to package instructions.

4. Serve noodles in bowls, pour hot broth over, and top with shredded chicken, cilantro, lime wedges, Thai basil, and bean sprouts.

Char Kway Teow (Malaysia)
Ingredients:

- 8 oz flat rice noodles
- 1/2 lb shrimp, peeled and deveined
- 1/2 lb Chinese sausage, sliced
- 2 eggs, beaten
- 1 cup bean sprouts
- 2 cloves garlic, minced
- 2 tbsp soy sauce
- 1 tbsp oyster sauce
- 1 tbsp dark soy sauce
- 1 tbsp sugar
- 1 tbsp vegetable oil
- 1 tbsp chili paste (optional)
- Green onions, chopped for garnish

Instructions:

1. Heat vegetable oil in a wok over high heat. Add garlic, Chinese sausage, and shrimp, and stir-fry until cooked.
2. Add the eggs and scramble them in the wok.
3. Stir in soy sauces, oyster sauce, sugar, and chili paste.

4. Add cooked rice noodles and toss everything together.

5. Garnish with bean sprouts and chopped green onions. Serve hot.

Yaki Soba (Japan)

Ingredients:

- 8 oz yakisoba noodles (or substitute with ramen noodles)
- 1/2 lb pork, thinly sliced
- 1/2 onion, sliced
- 1 carrot, julienned
- 1/2 cabbage, shredded
- 2 tbsp soy sauce
- 1 tbsp oyster sauce
- 1 tbsp ketchup
- 1 tbsp Worcestershire sauce
- 2 tbsp vegetable oil
- Pickled ginger and sesame seeds for garnish

Instructions:

1. Cook the yakisoba noodles according to package instructions.
2. Heat vegetable oil in a pan and sauté pork until browned. Add onion, carrot, and cabbage and cook until softened.
3. Stir in soy sauce, oyster sauce, ketchup, and Worcestershire sauce.
4. Add the cooked noodles to the pan and toss to combine.
5. Garnish with pickled ginger and sesame seeds. Serve hot.

Beef Noodle Soup (Taiwan)

Ingredients:

- 8 oz wheat noodles
- 1 lb beef shank or brisket
- 4 cups beef broth
- 1/4 cup soy sauce
- 1 tbsp rice wine
- 2 tbsp sugar
- 2 cloves garlic, minced
- 1-inch piece ginger, sliced
- 2-3 star anise
- 2 green onions, chopped
- Pickled mustard greens (optional)

Instructions:

1. In a pot, combine beef, beef broth, soy sauce, rice wine, sugar, garlic, ginger, and star anise. Bring to a boil, then reduce to a simmer for 2 hours until the beef is tender.
2. Cook the noodles according to package instructions.
3. Slice the beef thinly and add it to the broth.
4. Serve the noodles in bowls, ladle the beef broth over, and top with green onions and pickled mustard greens.

Noodle Soup with Pork (China)

Ingredients:

- 8 oz egg noodles
- 1/2 lb ground pork
- 4 cups chicken broth
- 1 tbsp soy sauce
- 1 tbsp rice wine
- 1/4 tsp five-spice powder
- 2 cloves garlic, minced
- 1-inch piece ginger, sliced
- 1/4 cup chopped green onions
- Sesame oil for garnish

Instructions:

1. In a pot, sauté garlic and ginger until fragrant. Add ground pork and cook until browned.
2. Add chicken broth, soy sauce, rice wine, and five-spice powder. Bring to a simmer and cook for 20 minutes.
3. Cook egg noodles according to package instructions.
4. Serve noodles in bowls, pour broth and pork over, and garnish with green onions and a drizzle of sesame oil.

Mie Ayam (Indonesia)

Ingredients:

- 8 oz egg noodles
- 1/2 lb chicken breast, cooked and shredded
- 2 tbsp soy sauce
- 1 tbsp oyster sauce
- 1 tbsp sesame oil
- 2 cloves garlic, minced
- 2 tbsp vegetable oil
- 1/4 cup fried shallots
- 1/4 cup chopped green onions
- 1 hard-boiled egg, halved

Instructions:

1. Cook egg noodles according to package instructions.
2. Heat vegetable oil in a pan and sauté garlic until fragrant. Add shredded chicken, soy sauce, oyster sauce, and sesame oil. Stir to coat.
3. Toss the cooked noodles with the chicken mixture.
4. Serve with fried shallots, chopped green onions, and a hard-boiled egg on top.

Baked Ziti (Italy)

Ingredients:

- 8 oz ziti pasta
- 2 cups marinara sauce
- 1/2 lb Italian sausage, crumbled
- 1 cup ricotta cheese
- 1 1/2 cups shredded mozzarella cheese
- 1/4 cup grated Parmesan cheese
- 2 cloves garlic, minced
- 1 tbsp olive oil
- 1/4 cup chopped basil

Instructions:

1. Cook ziti pasta according to package instructions.
2. In a pan, heat olive oil and sauté garlic and sausage until browned.
3. Add marinara sauce and simmer for 10 minutes.
4. In a baking dish, layer cooked ziti, ricotta, sausage sauce, and mozzarella. Repeat layers.
5. Top with Parmesan cheese and bake at 375°F for 20 minutes, or until bubbly.

Yakisoba (Japan)

Ingredients:

- 8 oz yakisoba noodles
- 1/2 lb pork, thinly sliced
- 1 onion, sliced
- 1 carrot, julienned
- 1/2 cabbage, shredded
- 2 tbsp soy sauce
- 1 tbsp Worcestershire sauce
- 1 tbsp ketchup
- 1 tbsp oyster sauce
- 1 tbsp vegetable oil
- Green onions for garnish

Instructions:

1. Cook yakisoba noodles according to package instructions.
2. Heat vegetable oil in a pan and sauté pork, onion, carrot, and cabbage until softened.
3. Stir in soy sauce, Worcestershire sauce, ketchup, and oyster sauce.
4. Add cooked noodles and toss everything together.
5. Garnish with green onions. Serve hot.

Sweet Soy Noodles (Indonesia)

Ingredients:

- 8 oz egg noodles
- 2 tbsp sweet soy sauce (kecap manis)
- 1 tbsp soy sauce
- 1 tbsp sesame oil
- 2 cloves garlic, minced
- 1/2 onion, sliced
- 1/2 cup shredded carrots
- 1/2 cup bean sprouts
- 2 green onions, chopped
- 1 egg (optional)
- Chili paste or sambal (optional for spice)

Instructions:

1. Cook the egg noodles according to the package instructions. Drain and set aside.
2. In a large skillet or wok, heat sesame oil over medium-high heat. Add garlic and onion, sautéing until fragrant and softened.
3. Add the carrots and cook for 2-3 minutes until tender.
4. Push the veggies to the side of the pan and scramble the egg (if using) in the same skillet.

5. Add the cooked noodles, sweet soy sauce, soy sauce, and chili paste (if using). Toss everything together to combine.

6. Stir in the bean sprouts and green onions, cooking for 1-2 minutes.

7. Serve the noodles hot, garnished with more green onions.

Stir-Fried Rice Noodles with Shrimp (Vietnam)
Ingredients:

- 8 oz rice noodles
- 1/2 lb shrimp, peeled and deveined
- 2 cloves garlic, minced
- 1/2 onion, sliced
- 1/2 bell pepper, sliced
- 1/4 cup fish sauce
- 1 tbsp sugar
- 1 tbsp soy sauce
- 1 tbsp oyster sauce
- 1 tbsp vegetable oil
- 1/4 cup cilantro, chopped
- 1 lime, cut into wedges

Instructions:

1. Cook the rice noodles according to package instructions. Drain and set aside.
2. In a wok or large skillet, heat vegetable oil over medium-high heat. Add garlic and onion, sautéing until softened.
3. Add the shrimp and cook for 2-3 minutes until they turn pink and opaque.
4. Add bell pepper, fish sauce, soy sauce, oyster sauce, and sugar. Stir to combine.

5. Add the cooked rice noodles to the skillet and toss everything together to coat evenly.

6. Cook for another 2 minutes, allowing the noodles to absorb the sauce.

7. Garnish with cilantro and serve with lime wedges on the side.

Khao Poon (Laos)
Ingredients:

- 8 oz rice noodles
- 1 lb chicken thighs, boneless and skinless
- 4 cups chicken broth
- 1 can coconut milk
- 1 tbsp red curry paste
- 1 tbsp fish sauce
- 1 tbsp sugar
- 2 cloves garlic, minced
- 1 onion, sliced
- 1/4 cup lime juice
- Fresh herbs (cilantro, mint) for garnish
- Bean sprouts for garnish

Instructions:

1. In a pot, bring chicken broth to a boil. Add the chicken thighs and cook for 25-30 minutes until tender.
2. Remove the chicken and shred it. Set the broth aside.
3. In a separate pan, heat a little oil and sauté garlic, onion, and red curry paste until fragrant.

4. Add the sautéed mixture to the chicken broth along with coconut milk, fish sauce, and sugar. Stir to combine and bring to a simmer.

5. Cook the rice noodles according to package instructions and divide them into serving bowls.

6. Pour the hot broth and chicken over the noodles.

7. Garnish with fresh herbs and bean sprouts. Serve with lime wedges.

Spaghetti Carbonara (Italy)

Ingredients:

- 8 oz spaghetti
- 1/2 lb pancetta or guanciale, diced
- 2 eggs
- 1/2 cup Parmesan cheese, grated
- 1/2 cup Pecorino Romano cheese, grated
- Freshly ground black pepper
- 2 cloves garlic, minced
- Salt, to taste

Instructions:

1. Cook the spaghetti according to the package instructions, reserving 1/2 cup of pasta water before draining.
2. In a skillet, cook pancetta or guanciale over medium heat until crispy. Add minced garlic and cook for 1 more minute.
3. In a bowl, whisk together the eggs, Parmesan, Pecorino, and a generous amount of black pepper.
4. Add the cooked pasta to the skillet with pancetta and garlic. Toss to coat in the rendered fat.
5. Remove from heat and slowly add the egg mixture, stirring quickly to prevent the eggs from scrambling.
6. Add pasta water as needed to achieve a creamy consistency.

7. Serve immediately with extra cheese and black pepper.

Guo Tie Noodles (China)

Ingredients:

- 8 oz wheat noodles
- 1/2 lb ground pork
- 1/4 cup soy sauce
- 1 tbsp rice wine
- 1/2 tsp sesame oil
- 1 tbsp ginger, minced
- 2 cloves garlic, minced
- 1/4 cup green onions, chopped
- 2 tbsp vegetable oil
- 1/2 cup cabbage, finely chopped
- Chili oil (optional)

Instructions:

1. Cook the wheat noodles according to the package instructions. Drain and set aside.

2. In a pan, heat vegetable oil over medium-high heat. Add ground pork, ginger, and garlic, sautéing until the pork is browned and cooked through.

3. Add soy sauce, rice wine, sesame oil, and cabbage. Stir and cook for 2-3 minutes until the cabbage wilts.

4. Add the cooked noodles to the pan and toss everything together.

5. Stir in green onions and chili oil if using.

6. Serve hot, garnished with additional green onions.

Noodle Soup with Fish Balls (Hong Kong)
Ingredients:

- 8 oz egg noodles
- 1/2 lb fish balls (store-bought or homemade)
- 4 cups chicken or fish broth
- 2 cloves garlic, minced
- 2-3 slices ginger
- 2 green onions, chopped
- 1 tbsp soy sauce
- 1 tbsp oyster sauce
- 1 tbsp sesame oil
- 1/4 cup bok choy or spinach
- Salt and pepper to taste
- Chili oil (optional)

Instructions:

1. Cook the egg noodles according to the package instructions. Drain and set aside.
2. In a pot, heat sesame oil over medium heat and sauté garlic and ginger until fragrant.
3. Add the broth, soy sauce, and oyster sauce. Bring to a boil, then lower the heat and simmer for 10-15 minutes.

4. Add the fish balls to the broth and cook for 5-7 minutes until they float to the surface.

5. Add the cooked noodles and bok choy to the soup. Stir to combine.

6. Serve hot, garnished with green onions and a drizzle of chili oil for heat (optional).

Singapore Noodles (Singapore)
 Ingredients:

- 8 oz rice vermicelli noodles
- 1/2 lb shrimp, peeled and deveined
- 1/2 bell pepper, thinly sliced
- 1/2 onion, thinly sliced
- 1/2 carrot, julienned
- 2 cloves garlic, minced
- 1 tbsp curry powder
- 1 tbsp soy sauce
- 1 tbsp oyster sauce
- 1 tbsp sesame oil
- 1 egg, lightly beaten
- 2 green onions, chopped
- Salt to taste

Instructions:

1. Cook the rice noodles according to package instructions, then drain and set aside.

2. In a wok or large pan, heat sesame oil over medium-high heat. Add garlic, bell pepper, onion, and carrot. Stir-fry for 2-3 minutes until softened.

3. Add shrimp and cook for 2-3 minutes until pink and opaque.

4. Push the shrimp and veggies to one side of the pan, and pour the beaten egg into the empty space. Scramble the egg until cooked through.

5. Add the cooked rice noodles, curry powder, soy sauce, and oyster sauce. Stir everything together to coat the noodles evenly.

6. Garnish with green onions and serve hot.

Xian Biang Biang Noodles (China)

Ingredients:

- 8 oz wide wheat noodles
- 1/2 lb ground pork
- 2 cloves garlic, minced
- 1 tbsp soy sauce
- 1 tbsp black vinegar
- 1 tbsp chili paste or oil
- 1 tbsp sesame oil
- 2 tbsp green onions, chopped
- 1/2 cup bok choy or spinach
- 1 tsp sugar
- Salt to taste

Instructions:

1. Cook the wheat noodles according to package instructions, then drain and set aside.

2. In a pan, heat sesame oil over medium-high heat. Add garlic and ground pork, sautéing until the pork is browned and fully cooked.

3. Add soy sauce, black vinegar, sugar, and chili paste or oil to the pork mixture. Stir to combine and cook for 2-3 minutes.

4. Add the bok choy or spinach and cook until wilted.

5. Toss the cooked noodles in the sauce, making sure to coat them evenly.

6. Garnish with chopped green onions and serve hot.

Kuy Teav Phnom Penh (Cambodia)

Ingredients:

- 8 oz rice noodles
- 1/2 lb beef or chicken, thinly sliced
- 4 cups beef or chicken broth
- 1 tbsp fish sauce
- 1 tbsp soy sauce
- 1/4 cup lime juice
- 2 cloves garlic, minced
- 1/2 onion, sliced
- Fresh herbs (cilantro, basil)
- Bean sprouts for garnish
- Chili paste (optional)

Instructions:

1. Cook the rice noodles according to package instructions, then drain and set aside.
2. In a pot, bring the broth to a boil. Add the sliced beef or chicken, cooking until fully cooked.
3. Add garlic, onion, fish sauce, soy sauce, and lime juice to the pot. Stir well.
4. Divide the noodles into serving bowls and pour the hot soup and meat over the noodles.

5. Garnish with fresh herbs, bean sprouts, and chili paste for a bit of heat (optional).

6. Serve hot.

Laksa Lemak (Malaysia)
Ingredients:

- 8 oz rice noodles
- 1/2 lb shrimp, peeled and deveined
- 1 tbsp red curry paste
- 1 can (14 oz) coconut milk
- 2 cups chicken broth
- 2 cloves garlic, minced
- 1/2 onion, sliced
- 1 tbsp fish sauce
- 1 tbsp lime juice
- 1 boiled egg, halved
- Fresh herbs (cilantro, mint)
- Bean sprouts for garnish
- Chili oil (optional)

Instructions:

1. Cook the rice noodles according to package instructions, then drain and set aside.

2. In a pot, heat a bit of oil and sauté garlic and onion until softened. Add red curry paste and cook for 1-2 minutes until fragrant.

3. Pour in the chicken broth and coconut milk. Bring to a boil, then lower the heat and simmer for 5-7 minutes.

4. Add shrimp to the soup and cook for 3-4 minutes until they turn pink and opaque.

5. Add fish sauce, lime juice, and season with salt to taste.

6. Divide the cooked noodles into bowls and ladle the soup over them.

7. Garnish with a boiled egg, fresh herbs, bean sprouts, and chili oil (if using).

8. Serve hot.